The
Will
of God

by
Betty Miller

First Edition Published 1980
Second Printing 1982
Third Printing 1983
Fourth Printing 1984
Fifth Printing 1987
Sixth Printing 1988
Seventh Printing 1989
Eighth Printing 1991
Ninth Printing 1994
Tenth Printing 2003
Print On Demand

The Will of God

ISBN 1-57149-004-3

CHRIST UNLIMITED MINISTRIES, INC.
Pastor R.S. "Bud" Miller - Publisher
P.O. Box 850
Dewey, Arizona 86327

Printed in U.S.A.

Scripture quotations are taken from the King James Version
unless otherwise indicated.

Contents

Preface

Greetings in the name of our Lord Jesus Christ:

I present this book to the body of Christ as the Holy Spirit presented it to me. I challenge you to allow God's Spirit of truth, and the Bible, to test the accuracy of the words within these pages. This book, part of the Overcoming Life Series, is also addressed to all seekers of truth who know not THE CHRIST UNLIMITED, as it would be my privilege to introduce you to Him.

During the early years of the ministry, I struggled to learn how to hear the voice of God. Once, while nervously waiting to speak before a large audience, and not being sure on what subject I should speak, I posed to the Lord in prayer this question: "Lord, what am I going to say to all these people?" In my spirit, I heard Him very clearly reply, "Betty, I was hoping you would not say anything, as I really wanted to speak." Yes, He wants to speak through us, as we yield to His Spirit. Submitting to the Lord and the guidance of the Holy Spirit, I found, was not only possible, but the only way He wants us to minister. **For it is not ye that speak, but the Spirit of your Father which speaketh in you (Matthew 10:20).**

This book is a gift from the Holy Spirit. I take no credit for it. If something within these pages blesses you, enlightens you, brings you closer to the Lord, releases you from fear or bondage, or heals or delivers you, then please lift your voice in praise to the precious Savior of our souls, Jesus Christ our Lord! On the other hand, if you find some of these things difficult to receive, hard to understand, or totally heretical from your viewpoint, would you also look to the Lord and ask Him if it could possibly be the truth? With an open and honest heart, will you ask God to change any pre-conceived ideas, and be free from traditions to receive of Him, His truth? His truth always brings freedom, never bondage. **And ye shall know the truth, and the truth shall make you free (John 8:32).**

In walking with the Lord, I have found we must obey the

things we feel He is speaking to us. In my personal life, I used to be fearful of speaking for the Lord because I was so afraid of missing Him and making mistakes. (He, of course, has now delivered me of all my fears. Praise Him!) He encouraged me not to quit because of mistakes when He spoke these words to me: "Betty, if I receive the glory and praise for all the things that are a blessing to people, I also receive the responsibility for your mistakes, as long as you are striving to please me. I am able to make even those work for your good." **And we know that all things work together for good to them that love God, to them who are the called according to his purpose (Romans 8:28).** We serve a wonderful, loving God, who encourages us to follow and obey Him that we might be blessed, and in turn bless others!

This book was written as an act of obedience to the Lord, whom I dearly love. I consider it an honor to write for Him. Years ago, when I was in prayer, the Lord spoke that I was to write a book, but I never felt it was God's timing, nor did I feel the unction or anointing to begin this work until now. Over the past year God has performed a series of miracles to confirm that it is now His time, and has made the arrangements for this to become a reality.

I pray that this book, along with the Overcoming Life Series, may help you learn to walk closer to our Lord, as He is THE CHRIST UNLIMITED!

I am, by His love,
A handmaiden of the Lord,

Betty Miller
February, 1980

> **If any man will do his will, he shall know of the doctrine, whether it be of God, or whether I speak of myself (John 7:17).**

Foreword

It just seemed natural that I would do the foreword on this book since my wife, Betty, and myself, are "one flesh." God, through the Holy Spirit, has given by revelation to Betty many truths of His Word, which have been set forth in this book.

The Lord spoke to Betty about ten years ago that she was to write a book for Him, and that He would arrange the right time and place to write it. Betty simply took this vision and set it aside until God began to "quicken" her spirit to bring it forth. One morning, very early, Betty awakened, and began to write as the Lord dictated to her. In giving her this small initial portion of the book, He showed her how, by submitting to His Spirit, and completely yielding to Him, He would feed to her the message He wanted to share with the body of Christ. He also revealed how quickly and easily it would be completed. The messages that God has given in this Overcoming Life Series are to all who desire to become "overcomers" and be "conformed to the image of His son" (**Romans 8:29**). Our Lord is not satisfied that a person remains a "babe" in Christ, but longs for each "babe" to grow to maturity. He desires that we should strive to become overcomers, live the overcoming life, and claim the promises of the inheritance of all things that are to be given to the overcomers.

I thank God that He has allowed me to share such close love and companionship with Betty. I know that within her heart she has no personal ambitions, no personal ends to achieve. Betty has simply been doing the will of the Father in the writing of this anointed book. May the Lord bless you with this book, as He has blessed us in being a part of His work.

Yours in Christ,

Pastor R.S. "Bud" Miller

He that overcometh shall inherit all things; and I will be his God and he shall be my son (Revelation 21:7).

Credits & Acknowledgments

ALL PRAISE AND CREDIT
GOES TO **THE CHRIST UNLIMITED!**

Truly Christ, the Father, and the Holy Spirit, are to be praised, not only for this book, but for our very lives. His sacrifice on Calvary made it possible to know Him and all the members of God's family.

As with the printing of any book, there are lots of people responsible for the words on these pages, physical words as well as spiritual words. All the people that have ever been a part of my life, all the people that have prayed and supported this ministry, my friends and my family have truly contributed to this work. Special credit should be given to my husband, Bud, whose faithful and loving prayers, encouragement, leadership, and love are a big part of this book. Also, to everyone whose books and articles I've read, to the ministers of the Gospel, whose sermons I've heard, I express my gratitude. For each has contributed, in some measure, to this book. The list is endless, but eternity has the records. So instead of naming individuals on this page and giving them earthly credit, I prefer the Lord Jesus Christ to reward them each as only He can. God bless you all, and may you be surprised as you open up the box that contains your heavenly treasures.

For the Son of man shall come in the glory of his Father with his angels; and then he shall reward every man according to his works (Matthew 16:27).

Introduction

THE WILL OF GOD shows you the first step to doing the will of God is in knowing the will of God. This book teaches you how to know the will of God for your personal life, your family, your ministry, and your finances. You will also find out why God allows sin, sickness, and suffering in the world.

There are spiritual laws governing both Divine and Satanic workings, and knowledge of these will give you the revelation as to the source of supernatural experiences. Satan is using deception to get believers to accept things that are not coming from God.

THE WILL OF GOD gives you the truth about what God does and does not do, so the believer is equipped with the necessary knowledge to resist the devil. If the believer does not have this discernment, he cannot take an attitude of resistance to a thing he believes is of God, thereby the enemy will prevail over him.

Many things people attribute to God's sovereignty are nothing else but the result of the Satanic world-ruler's work.

As overcomers, Christians are not supposed to suffer under many things which have been accepted as normal. God will never do anything outside of his Word and His character as shown in this book.

The Will of God

Ephesians 6:6: Not with eyeservice, as menpleasers;
But as the servants of Christ, doing the will of God
from the heart.

Logos and Rhema Agree

So many people want to know what the will of God is for
their lives. Often we hear statements such as the following, "If I
only knew what the will of God was for my life, I would do it."
Many sincere Christians seek God to know His will, yet they seem
to find no satisfactory answers. The reason for this is that there
are no pat answers aside from the Bible. The best definition for
the will of God would be that His Word is His will. If we find
anything in our lives that disagrees with His Word, then it is not
His will for us. On the other side of the coin, if we find anything in
His Word that is not in our lives, then it is His will that we receive
it.

To teach on the will of God in this light, we need to first
understand specifically what God's Word is. In the New Testament Greek, we have two meanings for the Word of God, "logos"
and "rhema." The first meaning for God's Word, "logos," denotes
The Word, a title of the Son of God. **In the beginning was the
Word, and the Word was with God, and the Word was God
(John 1:1); And the Word was made flesh, and dwelt among
us, (and we beheld his glory, the glory as of the only begotten
of the Father,) full of grace and truth (John 1:14).**

"Logos" also denotes the sayings or statements made by God,
the written Word, contained in the Bible. **2 Timothy 3:16-17**
says: **All Scripture is given by inspiration of God, and is prof-
itable for doctrine, for reproof, for correction, for instruction
in righteousness: That the man of God may be perfect, thor-**

1

oughly furnished unto all good works. By this verse we can see that God's Word (His Will) produces a perfect man. So, if we walk according to the Bible, we will do His perfect will.

The other meaning for the Word of God, "rhema," is the Word spoken to our spirits. **John 6:63** states, **It is the spirit that quickeneth; the flesh profiteth nothing: the words that I speak unto you, they are spirit, and they are life**. The first Word, "logos," is the reference to the whole written Word of God, while the Word, "rhema," is the individual Scripture which the Spirit brings to our remembrance for use in the time of need, or the voice we hear in our spirits when the Lord is speaking to us. "Rhema" can come also in the form of prophecy. When it does, it is alive to us and is quickened to our spirits. All "rhema" words should agree with the "logos" words.

Prophetic words should be tested the same way we test or prove other things that come to us. We must never build our lives on a prophecy or vision. The Lord generally uses prophecy to confirm those things He has already spoken to us. He generally does not bring guidance through a prophetic word. If He does, it will be easily entreated and we will have a witness in our hearts that it is the Lord speaking to us. We must always be guided by the Holy Spirit and His Word, and only seldom through either prophecies or ''fleeces.''

Why Not "Fleece" as Gideon Did?

What are "fleeces?" This term refers to a method of seeking God recorded in the Old Testament. In the book of Judges we find a man named Gideon who sought God's guidance in an unusual way. He was a warrior against Israel's enemies and a judge of Israel. The Midianites and the Amalekites had come to do battle against him. Since he was a man called of God, the Lord had already spoken to him about this battle and told him he would smite the Midianites (**Judges 6:16**). Gideon started to doubt God when the enemy began coming against him. (We are still like that

2

today.) He began a discourse with the Lord that is recorded in **Judges 6:36-40**:

And Gideon said unto God, If thou wilt save Israel by mine hand, as thou hast said, Behold, I will put a fleece of wool in the floor; and if the dew be on the fleece only, and it be dry upon all the earth beside, then shall I know that thou wilt save Israel by mine hand, as thou hast said. And it was so: for he rose up early on the morrow, and thrust the fleece together, and wringed the dew out of the fleece, a bowl full of water. And Gideon said unto God, Let not thine anger be hot against me, and I will speak but this once: let me prove, I pray thee, but this once with the fleece; let it now be dry only upon the fleece, and upon all the ground let there be dew. And God did so that night: for it was dry upon the fleece only, and there was dew on all the ground.

Gideon knew that it was wrong to test God, as he asked the Lord not to be angry with him for asking a second time and proposing this test for God.

Often people today propose the same "fleeces" to God by saying, "God, if you will do 'so and so', I will do 'such and such'; or, "If you will cause a certain thing to happen, God, I will know it is your will for me to do a certain thing." We should not tempt God with such proposals because we have His Spirit within to guide us. We should not allow the circumstances about us to do the guiding, for Satan can create the situation we are proposing and thus divert us into believing it is God. God does, however, at times use circumstances to guide us, but they will be of His choosing and not ours. He arranges not only our outward circumstances, but also our inward circumstances, when leading us in the direction we are to go. The situations God arranges will always agree with His Word. We must test both circumstances and situations to see if God is initiating them or if the enemy is, lest we be tossed about with the blowing winds of fate. Mature Christians will never be victims of circumstance, but will have the mind of Christ and be moved by His Spirit in their affairs. Proposing "fleeces" unto the Lord shows our immaturity. When we are "babes" in Christ, the Lord will usually honor us in our requests, as we do not yet fully know how to receive His guidance. He will answer us even as He did Gideon. However, He does not want us to continue to seek our guidance in such a manner, and if we persist in doing it, we may become a victim of the devil and get "fleeced" ourselves. Let us be led of the Spirit and lined up with the Word of God so we do not miss His will for us. We will then know the Word, both "logos" and "rhema."

However, knowing the Word is not enough. There are people who have memorized the Bible and have a "head knowledge" of it, but do not have a "heart knowledge" of the Word. We must let the Word take root in our hearts for it to be effective in our lives. Our heart attitude toward God and our relationship with Jesus determine our course with God. If we continue to fellowship with God, we will be able to say with the Psalmist, David, **I delight to do thy will, O my God: yea, thy law is within my heart** (**Psalm 40:8**).

New Birth Brings a New Life

The first step is coming to know the Lord and experiencing the "new birth." When we receive the Son of God as our Saviour, we are given many promises. Let us look at one of those promises in **1 John 5:11-15**:

And this is the record, that God hath given to us eternal life, and this life is in his Son. He that hath the Son hath life; and he that hath not the Son of God hath not life. These things have I written unto you that believe on the name of the Son of God; that ye may know that ye have eternal life, and that ye may believe on the name of the Son of God. And this is the confidence that we have in him, that, if we ask any thing according to his will, he heareth us: And if we know that he hear us, whatsoever we ask, we know that we have the petitions that we desired of him.

He tells us that if we ask anything according to His will, He hears us and will answer.

Why then are we not receiving the answers to our prayers? Either we do not know what God's will is in regard to a specific situation, or we do not know the conditions through which God works. (Both His will and His conditions for receiving are found in His Word.) We must meet certain conditions and abide by certain principles if we are to receive the blessings of God and the desires of our hearts.

We could compare this to owning and driving a car. We can own a car, yet, if we do not know how to drive it, it would be of no benefit to us. We can also know the Word, yet not know how to apply it with the same result. In order to drive an automobile we must also follow certain rules, or we will end up in a collision. This also holds true with walking in God's will. We must follow certain rules, or we too will end up in a "wreck." It will not be God's fault if our prayers are not answered, but will be our own; we must be aware of the rules and we must follow them if we are to live the overcoming and victorious Christian life.

One of the first rules in the Christian walk is that we need to make a total commitment to God. Many "faith failures" occur because the first rules have been omitted or subsequent rules left out. Numerous people have experienced "spiritual wrecks" because of this, even though they have prayed for a certain thing with great faith. Their prayers remained unanswered because other requirements besides faith were also necessary. Satan uses these unanswered prayers to try and discourage them. He attempts to place the blame on God, thus destroying their total faith in Him.

By looking at God's Word we are able to discern many things that are obviously God's will that can be asked for confidently. We know that the Lord wants to heal us and that it is always His will to do so. **3 John 2** reads, **Beloved, I wish above all things that thou mayest prosper and be in health, even as thy soul prospereth. I Thessalonians 5:23 reads, And the very God of peace sanctify you wholly; and I pray God your whole spirit** and soul and body be preserved blameless unto the coming of our Lord Jesus Christ. Also, in **Luke 11** we find in the Lord's prayer that He said, **Thy will be done, as in heaven, so in earth**. There is no sickness in heaven, so we know it is His will that there be no sickness in earth. He wants us whole: spirit, soul and body.

When Jesus walked this earth, He went about healing all those that were ill when they came to Him. Now that He has returned to heaven, He has sent the Holy Spirit to continue the things He was doing while He walked the earth. We now have access to the power of the Holy Spirit which enables us to perform the same miracles that Jesus performed. What a glorious truth we need to receive in our hearts!

He is not willing for any to perish and go to hell. (**2 Peter 3:9, The Lord is not slack concerning his promise, as some men count slackness; but is longsuffering to usward, not willing that any should perish, but that all should come to repentance**.) He is also not willing that any be sick. Everyone will not accept God's gift of salvation, just as everyone will not accept God's atoning blood for healing. Some people, even after hearing God's healing message, still continue to believe the lies of the enemy and think it is not for today or believe it is not God's will for them to be healed as they are "suffering for Christ." We are not called to suffer for Christ with sickness.

Suffering for Christ

True suffering for Christ is always by choice. It involves laying down our lives for others. Jesus' suffering and death on the cross is the greatest example of suffering for others. He said in **John 10:17-18, Therefore doth my Father love me, because I lay down my life, that I might take it again. No man taketh it from me, but I lay it down of myself. I have power to lay it down, and I have power to take it again. This commandment have I received of my Father**. Jesus suffered because He chose to do so. Paul is another example of willful suffering for Christ, as he too chose to suffer. He could have refused, but rather chose to go to Jerusalem, even though it was prophesied over him that bonds and affliction awaited him. **Acts 21:13** records his reply as the Holy Ghost, speaking through Agabus, told of his fate; **Then Paul answered, What mean ye to weep and to break mine heart? for I am ready not to be bound only, but also to die at Jerusalem for the name of the Lord Jesus.**

How do we suffer for Christ today? We suffer for Christ by staying in a hard place, rather than fleeing, in hopes that redemption might come to those that misunderstand us. We suffer for Christ when we choose to fast instead of eat; when we leave our comfortable homes and go to mission fields that are filthy and pagan; when we turn the other cheek; when we pay a bill that is not our own; when we ''go the second mile''; when we rise at the midnight hour to pray; and when we minister to others when it is not convenient for us. There are many forms of suffering that are just as valid as the stripes Paul bore for the Lord's sake. We can endure emotional and physical pain as we give up the things we could have in this world for the kingdom of God's sake.

However, suffering with sickness is not a form of suffering for Christ, as Jesus paid the price on Calvary not only for our sin, but also for our sickness. The word in the Greek, "sozo," is used interchangeably to mean "to save" and "to heal" throughout the New Testament. He does not want us to keep our sickness any more than He wants us to keep our sin. If He paid for it on the cross, then we do not have to bear it today. (**Isaiah 53:5, But he was wounded for our transgressions, he was bruised for our iniquities: the chastisement of our peace was upon him; and with his stripes we are healed.**)

Perhaps one of the things that causes us to think that God is behind all suffering is that we do not understand the different forms of suffering. (Keep in mind the Greek word for suffering means to "bear" or "endure.")

When we first come to the Lord, most of our suffering is because we have broken spiritual and physical laws. Therefore, we are suffering as a result of these broken laws. This form of suffering comes upon the Christian and the non-Christian alike. However, if we walk with the Lord He will lead us out of this kind of suffering as it is the result of sin. Jesus suffered on the cross to relieve us of this. Types of this suffering would be sickness, depression, fear, poverty, filth, torment, emotional pain stemming from divorce or broken relationships, anxiety, loneliness, grief, stress, disorder, confusion, etc.

Other forms of suffering are seen in those Christians who live godly lives, and due to this, they suffer the abuse of those who falsely accuse them. Their flesh aches as they resist the temptations of sin; they leave family and friends because their hearts hurt to take the message of Christ to others; and some suffer being "unequally yoked" with unsaved mates.

1 Peter 4:15-16 says: **But let none of you suffer as a murderer, or as a thief, or as an evildoer, or as a busybody in other men's matters. Yet if any man suffer as a Christian, let him not be ashamed; but let him glorify God on this behalf**.

Verse 19 states, **Wherefore let them that suffer according to the will of God commit the keeping of their souls to him in well doing, as unto a faithful Creator**.

When we do not have sufficient knowledge to discern between suffering under Satan's hand and enduring for Christ's sake, we can be deceived by the devil to accept things that the Lord would not have us bear.

A good way to deal with problems of this nature would be to approach them with a submissive attitude before the Lord, and ask Him to reveal what He would have us do. **James 4:7-8** states, **Submit yourselves therefore to God. Resist the devil, and he will flee from you. Draw nigh to God, and he will draw nigh to you. Cleanse your hands, ye sinners; and purify your hearts, ye double minded**.

Many honest and sincere Christians have faithfully followed the first half of **verse 7**, but have neglected the second by not really resisting the devil. They have become double-minded (believing something from Satan to be from God), and the devil has been able to put needless suffering on them.

If we would voice our prayer to God in the following way this could be avoided: "Father, I come to You in Jesus' name. I willingly submit to do all that You ask of me, and will endure and bear all that You place before me, but I will not receive those things that the devil would put upon me. I yield to You, Lord, and if You want me to continue suffering I am willing, for I know You will give me abundant grace; but I resist the devil and the abuses he would put upon me."

If God calls us to endure something, He will always give us the peace, grace, and strength to pass through it victoriously. However, if the devil is behind it, it will drain us, destroy our peace, and eventually overcome us.

Many people who endure sickness, thinking it is suffering for the Lord, eventually die agonizing deaths, leaving families with enormous doctor bills and drained emotions. In no way can this be the Lord.

Many of us have endured situations that were not God's will because of a lack of knowledge of God's Word. We have not understood the Lord's ways nor our rights in Christ; therefore we have suffered many failures. **My people are destroyed for lack of knowledge: because thou hast rejected knowledge, I will also reject thee... (Hosea 4:6).**

We should not allow the devil to condemn us over past failures that occurred when we did not have the light, but should seek God today for today's victories.

Our God is a God of victory! The only way God can get glory from our illnesses is that we be healed. Then we can declare the mercy of the Great Physician to others. We can witness to the healing power of God and thereby glorify His name.

Jesus never had any sickness in His body. He suffered, but never with sickness. **Though he were a Son, yet learned he obedience by the things which he suffered; And being made perfect, he became the author of eternal salvation unto all them**

9

that obey him. (**Hebrews 5:8-9**). Jesus is our example. We should not look at other people and their experiences, but should keep our eyes on the Lord and seek to be like Him. If He was not sick, then we should not suffer with sickness.

What kind of suffering did Jesus endure? He was a perfect man so we know it was not for sin, but rather because He did not sin. He resisted the pull of the flesh and its desires rather than sin against God. The appetites of our flesh must be overcome through suffering and by not yielding to desires that are contrary to God's will. We can see that this kind of suffering involves an act of our will. We make a choice to suffer rather than displease the Lord.

The highest kind of suffering is sharing in the sufferings of Christ. We are told in **Philippians 1:29, For unto you it is given in the behalf of Christ, not only to believe on Him, but also to suffer for his sake**. This form of suffering comes only as we make the choice to follow completely in the footsteps of Jesus. It involves a total dying to self and a daily crucifixion to our way with full surrender to His. Paul chose this path and ultimately became an overcomer entering into the fullness of God's Sonship. This is the destiny for all who choose to identify with Christ in His sufferings.

It will not be burdensome to submit ourselves to this suffering, if we keep in mind the prize in store for all those who follow in His steps. **It is a faithful saying: For if we be dead with him, we shall also live with him; if we suffer, we shall also reign with him; If we deny him, he also will deny us. (2 Timothy 2:11-12)**. We shall rule and reign with Him when He comes back to this earth, if we suffer with Him. It will not be the entire body of Christ that does the ruling and reigning, but those who have been conformed to His image, and have, in this life, learned to rule and reign. **That I may know Him, and the power of his resurrection, and the fellowship of his sufferings, being made conformable unto his death...I press toward the mark for the prize of the high calling of God in Christ Jesus (Philippians 3:10 and 14).**

10

This high calling demands our all, and we will make up the sufferings that are lacking in the body of Christ, even as Paul did. **Even now I rejoice in the midst of my sufferings on your behalf. And in my own person I am making up whatever is still lacking and remains to be completed (on our part) of Christ's afflictions, for the sake of His body, which is the church. (Colossians 1:24** AMP). We find that the path that leads to kingship with the Lord comes by suffering.

When two of the disciples came to Jesus and desired a place of rulership with Him, we find that His answer in **Mark 10:37-40** clearly pointed to this truth. **They said unto him, Grant unto us that we may sit, one on thy right hand, and the other on thy left hand, in thy glory. But Jesus said unto them, Ye know not what ye ask: can ye drink of the cup that I drink of? and be baptized with the baptism that I am baptized with? And they said unto him, We can. And Jesus said unto them, Ye shall indeed drink of the cup that I drink of; and with the baptism that I am baptized withal shall ye be baptized: But to sit on my right hand and on my left hand is not mine to give; but it shall be given to them for whom it is prepared.**

The overcomers will be baptized with a baptism of suffering just as Jesus was, but just as Jesus was able to endure the cross for the joy that was set before Him, the overcomers will also go through suffering with that same grace and joy.

Looking unto Jesus the author and finisher of our faith; who for the joy that was set before him endured the cross, despising the shame, and is set down at the right hand of the throne of God. (Hebrews 12:2).

We can see the three forms of suffering are as follows: (1) Suffering because of sin and selfishness; (2) Suffering on the behalf of others; (3) Suffering for Christ. In **Matthew 13**, we find a parable about the sower and the seed. In reading this parable we find that Christians bring forth fruit in their lives, some thirtyfold, some sixtyfold, and some a hundredfold. Paralleling this parable with this teaching on suffering we can see that some Christians are still thirtyfold (involved in self, or carnal Christians), others are sixtyfold (living for others), and some have come to the hundredfold dimension of "making up what is lacking in Christ's afflictions."

Serving God and doing His will ultimately leads us into suffering with Him. Understanding this form of suffering can help us to walk as obedient servants of the Lord. Perhaps other areas we need to cover are those of Job's sufferings and Paul's "thorn in the flesh." These will help us to fully separate our own sufferings from those sufferings that are truly for Christ's sake.

Job's Suffering

Some people blame all their misfortunes on God and then say they are suffering just like Job. However, we never see them get the victory that Job got. The last chapter in the book of Job clearly shows us that Job came out of his trial and was restored for all that he lost. The Word says that the latter end of Job was blessed more than his beginning. Why did Job go through his trial? Did God send the evil or was it Satan?

If we look closely at chapter one, we find that we are viewing a heavenly scene as well as an earthly one. First, Job is spoken of as a perfect man that feared God and shunned evil. We are told that he was a very wealthy man with much substance. He was continually offering sacrifices to God for himself and his children. Then the scene shifts and we see Satan coming before God in heaven. (We need to keep in mind this is taking place before Jesus' victory over Satan at the cross at which time Satan was cast out of heaven. He still had access to visit heaven although he had been walking up and down on the face of the earth. See **Revelation 12**.)

The Lord is pleased with Job and tells Satan that there is not another man like him on the earth. Satan then says to God that Job is only serving Him because he has been blessed by Him. If Job lost all that he had, says Satan, then he would curse God.

The Lord then replies to Satan in **Job 1:12, Behold, all that he hath is in thy power; only upon himself put not forth thine hand. So Satan went forth from the presence of the Lord.**

Satan then began an onslaught of tragedies against Job. First, his servants were killed with the sword, then fire destroyed his sheep and more servants. Next, his camels were carried away, and his sons and daughters were killed in a windstorm. But even after all that, Job did not sin nor charge God foolishly, but rather worshipped God.

In **chapter 2** we return to the heavenly scene and find Satan making another appearance before the Lord. The Lord then speaks of Job as still being an upright man that feareth God. Satan then says to God that if Job is afflicted in his flesh, then he will curse God. **The Lord said unto Satan, Behold, he is in thy hand; but save his life. So went Satan forth from the presence of the Lord, and smote Job with sore boils from the sole of his foot unto his crown (Job 2:6-7).** Job's wife then tried to get him to curse God and die, yet Job replied, **What? shall we receive good at the hand of God, and shall we not receive evil? In all this did not Job sin with his lips (Job 2:10).**

Now let us notice some things before we go any further. First, we can see by this Scripture evil did not come from God, but it was Satan who came and brought all the afflictions. He sent death, a windstorm (many Christians blame storms on the Lord), fighting, destruction which resulted in the loss of Job's material property, and finally sickness. We can clearly see where sickness comes from by looking at this chapter; Satan is the bearer of it.

When Satan said to the Lord in **verse 5** to put forth His hand and touch Job's bone and flesh, the Lord replied in **verse 6**, he is in thine hand. The sickness didn't come from the hand of God, but obviously Satan's hand.

Why was Job in Satan's hand if he was a perfect man? God always sees His children as perfect because of their faith in Him. When we are committed to the Lord, he looks past our faults and failures. He did this with Job. He saw the true Job and knew that one day Job would recognize his self-righteousness and pride, and repent. In the meantime, the Lord spoke words of faith about Job to the devil. Because of God's omniscience, He sees the end and He knew that Job's perfection would one day be obtained by him. In **verse 9 and 10** we begin to get a clue as to Job's real problem which opened the door to the power of Satan. His wife mentions that he is retaining his integrity (self-righteousness); shortly thereafter, when he cannot understand what is happening to him, he begins to blame God for his misfortunes even as so many do today. **Verse 10** says he did not sin with his lips, but what was in Job's heart?

As we continue this narrative, we find there were several things in Job's heart that opened the door to the enemy. In **chapter 3 verse 25** we find that he had the sin of fear present in his heart. **For the thing which I greatly feared is come upon me, and that which I was afraid of is come unto me**. Fear is not of God. **Revelation 21:8** tells us, **But the fearful, and unbelieving, and the abominable, and murderers, and whoremongers, and sorcerers, and idolaters, and all liars, shall have their part in the lake which burneth with fire and brimstone: which is the second death.**

Many Christians today are allowing fear to rule them instead of trusting God, and just as Job's fears became manifest, so will the fears of those Christians be manifested who do not resist it, but allow fear to govern and rule them.

As we continue, we find the next sin that appears is that of self-pity which leads to thoughts of suicide (Chapter 6). Then as we progress, we begin to see Job's double-mindedness appearing. One minute, he is defending God and His goodness; the next, he is attributing evil to God. We also begin to see more and more of his self-righteousness and egotism as he defends his own worth before his friends. He refuses any of their advice as he "knows it all." (Although his friends' hearts are not right before God due to their lack of compassion and understanding, they have spoken some truths to Job.)

Job continues throughout the book to maintain his own righteousness and integrity instead of seeking it in the light of God's righteousness. He stands before God telling of all the good works and deeds he has done. Many today really believe, as Job did, that they are in right standing with God because their works are good, but they fail to see the pride of their own hearts. It was not God who allowed Satan to attack Job, but rather Job's own sin that opened the door for the attack. We see in **Job 2:6** the Lord replying to Satan that Job was already in Satan's hand, thus showing Job out of God's will, **And the Lord said unto Satan, Behold, he is in thine hand; but save his life.**

Finally in **Chapter 42**, Job's sin of self-righteousness is exposed, and he repents.

Then Job answered the Lord, and said, I know that thou canst do everything, and that no thought can be withholden from thee. Who is he that hideth counsel without knowledge? therefore have I uttered that I understood not; things too wonderful for me, which I knew not. Hear, I beseech thee, and I will speak: I will demand of thee, and declare thou unto me. I have heard of thee by the hearing of the ear: but now mine eye seeth thee. Wherefore I abhor myself, and repent in dust and ashes (Job 42:1-6).

Job knew of God but he really didn't get a God-centered spiritual vision until he ceased to be self-centered. Once this change of center occurred his spiritual eyes were opened to see Him. Then he knew that God was not his problem, but wickedness within his own heart had brought his tragedies. Immediately after he repented, the Lord restored unto him and blessed him with more than he had in the beginning.

We need not go through tragedies to learn the lesson Job learned. We can cry out unto God for a heart cleansing and He will show us the things in our lives that need to be cleansed. We can learn by two different means. We can learn by hearing and obeying, or we can learn by trial and error. If we hear and obey, we need not go through bad experiences to discover the truth.

15

Some people declare they learned a lot through their tragedies. The same lessons, however, could have been learned by studying the Word of God, and then obeying it. For example, I do not have to learn the truth of the following Proverb through actual transgression, ...**the way of transgressors is hard (Proverb 13:15)**. I can simply believe that it is the truth, and commit no transgression. If I choose to disbelieve this verse and sin, I will find out the "hard way" that the way of the transgressor is hard. The Lord would have us believe His Word and obey it.

Paul's "Thorn"

What about Paul's "thorn in the flesh"? Was it a sickness that the Lord refused to take away, yet gave him the grace to live with? Let us look at **2 Corinthians 12:7-11**.

And lest I should be exalted above measure through the abundance of the revelations, there was given to me a thorn in the flesh, the messenger of Satan to buffet me, lest I should be exalted above measure. For this thing I besought the Lord thrice, that it might depart from me. And he said unto me, My grace is sufficient for thee: for my strength is made perfect in weakness. Most gladly therefore will I rather glory in my infirmities, that the power of Christ may rest upon me. Therefore I take pleasure in infirmities, in reproaches, in necessities, in persecutions, in distresses for Christ's sake: for when I am weak, then am I strong. I am become a fool in glorying; ye have compelled me: for I ought to have been commended of you: for in nothing am I behind the very chiefest apostles, though I be nothing.

One guideline for interpreting the Bible is that it interprets itself through other Scriptures which contain similar words, phrases or subjects. In the present case, let us see how the Word of God defines a "thorn in the flesh." In the above Scripture, immediately following the mention of the thorn, it interprets itself as, "the messenger of Satan to buffet me." From this we can see that the

16

thorn was someone with an evil spirit who was speaking against Paul. A messenger is someone that speaks. He was receiving a buffeting or a tongue-lashing from someone contending against him. Buffeting could not possibly be sickness as buffeting comes from without. We can see this in the way the wind would buffet a ship in a storm.

Also by looking at the Word of God in **Joshua 23:13**, we can see one way that the Bible defines thorns.

Know for a certainty that the Lord your God will no more drive out any of these nations from before you; but they shall be snares and traps unto you, and scourges in your sides, and thorns in your eyes, until ye perish from off this good land which the Lord your God hath given you.

Paralleling this in **Ezekiel 28:24** we find the following: **And there shall be no more a pricking brier unto the house of Israel, nor any grieving thorn of all that are round about them, that despised them; and they shall know that I am the Lord God**.

From these three Scriptures then, we find that a "thorn in the flesh" would be a wicked person that would persecute another. Even today we refer to someone that harasses us as a "thorn in our side." Paul was seeking the Lord to remove this person from his life, but the Lord spoke to Paul and told him the person would remain, but He would give him the grace to bear the persecution and affliction from that individual.

Why didn't God remove that person from his life? Paul says this was because he was having such an abundance of revelations and visions that if everything had been going too smoothly, he would have been overcome by a spirit of pride. This spirit of pride was a weak area in Paul's life that needed to be overcome. We can see it throughout his writings, emerging time and time again. In **verse 11** of this Scripture we see him stating the fact that he was equal to the "chiefest apostles." The Lord knew if everything was fine for Paul, he could not handle the pride. Already miracles were happening in his ministry, so this "thorn in the flesh" was left until he could conquer the pride element.

Keep in mind that the Scriptures do not say that he kept this "thorn in the flesh" for the rest of his days. In fact, we see that he eventually overcame for he states in **2 Timothy 3:11, Persecutions, afflictions, which came unto me at Antioch, at Iconium, at Lystra; what persecutions I endured: but out of them all the Lord delivered me**. His "thorn in the flesh" troubled him only until he became an overcomer; after humility had been worked in Paul's life, he no longer was hurt or pricked by this thorn as his flesh had been crucified. **1 Peter 5:10** says, **But the God of all grace, who hath called us unto his eternal glory by Christ Jesus, after that ye have suffered awhile, make you perfect, stablish, strengthen, settle you**.

Paul's "Infirmities"

Some people are confused over his statement in which he says that he will take pleasure in his infirmities. What is Paul saying here? The Greek meaning for the word "infirmities" has a much broader meaning than our English word. It means any physical or moral weakness, a lack of strength or an inability to produce results.

With this knowledge in mind, we know that Paul is saying, "When I am weak, the Lord makes me strong; when I cannot do something, He makes me able to do it. He overcomes through me, and when I cannot handle the person who is persecuting me, God will give me the grace to bear it."

From this we see that the only reason God allows things to remain in our lives for a time is so that we can overcome them. He does not mean for them to be permanent. **Psalm 34:19** declares, **Many are the afflictions of the righteous: but the Lord delivereth him out of them all**.

If we follow in the Lord's steps we shall have persecution and suffering which will come through others; however, the Lord will always give us the opportunity to be victorious over them all. The suffering that the Lord speaks of is not that of sickness, fear, anxiety, depression, poverty, etc. that stem from our old carnal nature. The righteous are to suffer and be grieved over others, bearing others' physical and financial burdens, the untruth of their mouths, and their false accusations, etc. The Scripture verifies this in **1Peter 2:21-24** where Peter says:

For even hereunto were ye called: because Christ also suffered for us, leaving us an example, that ye should follow his steps: Who did no sin, neither was guile found in his mouth: Who, when he was reviled, reviled not again; when he suffered, he threatened not; but committed himself to him that judgeth righteously: Who his own self bare our sins in his own body on the tree, that we, being dead to sins, should live unto righteousness: by whose stripes ye were healed.

If Jesus took stripes on his back for our healing, then we need to receive that healing today and not allow the devil to convince us we are suffering for Christ. The Lord wants us whole: spirit, soul and body. This is His will and His Word.

Following Christ

Now that we can see His Word is His will, if we have any questions whether something is God's will or not, all we need to do is check to see what the Word says about it. If we have no access to His Word in a Bible, He will lead us by His Spirit. The first century Christians didn't have Bibles as we do today yet many led overcoming lives. If it is in His Word, then we can be assured that it is His will. If not, we need to put it away from us.

However, there are many things that are not specifically condoned or condemned in the Word. Also, there are things that we personally need answers about such as, "Is this the right mate for me? Should I move to another city? Should we purchase this house, car, etc.? Is it time to go out in a full-time ministry for the Lord?" and many more. How do we find the will of God about such matters?

Let us look to **Romans 12:1-3** for a basic pattern of being in God's will: **I beseech you therefore, brethren, by the mercies of God, that ye present your bodies a living sacrifice, holy, acceptable unto God, which is your reasonable service. And be not conformed to this world: but be ye transformed by the renewing of your mind, that ye may prove what is that good, and acceptable, and perfect, will of God. For I say, through the grace given unto me, to every man that is among you, not to think of himself more highly than he ought to think; but to think soberly, according as God hath dealt to every man the measure of faith**.

Our first step, and all future steps, for being in God's will will always have us present ourselves as a living sacrifice unto God.

Perhaps a better rendering for **verse 1** is found in the Amplified Version of the Bible. It reads:

I appeal to you therefore, brethren, and beg of you in view of (all) the mercies of God, to make a decisive dedication of your bodies -- presenting all your members and faculties -- as a living sacrifice, holy (devoted, consecrated) and well pleasing to God, which is your reasonable (rational, intelligent) service and spiritual worship. If we want to know what God's will is in any given situation, we first must be totally committed to Him; then we may expect to receive an answer from Him. A half-hearted commitment will inevitably bring confusion and ruin. If this foundation of total commitment is not laid first, then anything that we build on top will eventually crumble.

Let us look at a parable in **Luke 14:26-33** that verifies this:

If any man come to me, and hate not his father, and mother, and wife, and children, and brethren, and sisters, yea, and his own life also, he cannot be my disciple. And whosoever doth not bear his cross, and come after me, cannot be my disciple. For which of you, intending to build a tower, sitteth not down first, and counteth the cost, whether he have sufficient to finish it? Lest haply, after he hath laid the founda-

tion, and is not able to finish it, all that behold it begin to mock him, Saying, This man began to build, and was not able to finish. Or what king, going to make war against another king, sitteth not down first, and consulteth whether he be able with ten thousand to meet him that cometh against him with twenty thousand? Or else, while the other is yet a great way off, he sendeth an ambassage, and desireth conditions of peace. So likewise, whosoever he be of you that forsaketh not all that he hath, he cannot be my disciple.

Looking at these verses we notice the Lord Jesus is using a very strong word in **verse 26**, that is if we do not hate our father, mother, wife, children, brethren, and sisters and our own lives when we come to Him, we cannot be His disciple.

This does not mean we are to hate in the sense of despising and being unkind to them, but rather the meaning in the Greek for this particular word "hate" is in the sense of indifference to, or relative disregard for them in comparison with our attitude toward the Lord. We must not put our loved ones or our love for self ahead of our love for God. He demands first place in our lives above all else.

Yielding to the Cross

The only way for us to overcome is to bear our cross. What does this mean? Jesus was nailed to a cross for our sins, so if we follow in His steps, we too will be nailed to our own individual cross. Our cross will not be the one Jesus bore, or the one Paul bore, or even the ones other saints have borne, but we will bear the one intended solely for us. If we want to be a disciple we will have to bear our cross. We must identify with Christ's crucifixion.

That cross is the dying to self-will and henceforth living in the will of God. We will not count our lives dear, but will willingly give up all to follow the one we love. Each time we yield to self, we come down from our cross and refuse to bear it. When the work of the cross is finished in our lives, we will truly be dead to our way and desire only to live to His way. This work is a process, and the Holy Spirit will do this in us as quickly as we allow Him to do so. Since none of us like to die, we usually resist our cross.

Just as Jesus prayed an agonizing prayer in the Garden of Gethsemane as He yielded to the cross that awaited Him, we too will come to that place of agony where we must choose to die to our way and follow His. After we choose His way, then we will find that just as men nailed Jesus to His cross, men will nail us to ours. We must be like Jesus when this happens to us, and just as He prayed, **Father, forgive them; for they know not what they do...** (**Luke 23:34**), we too should offer forgiveness to those who hurt us and persecute us.

None of us can even know the will of God until we are willing to follow Him regardless of what that will is. Most Christians offer their plans to God for approval, instead of seeking to know God's plan for their lives. We have been exposed to popular teachings which teach that we follow God to get the things we desire of Him. It is no wonder there are so many "faith failures" when new Christians are taught that they can have the things of the world and the things of Jesus too.

Jesus taught that we must be willing to lose all to gain Him. He did not teach we could have anything we wanted if we followed Him. **Verse 33** of **Luke 14** tells us we must forsake all or we cannot be His disciple. We must be willing to give up our comfortable homes, our businesses, our successes and worldly esteem, our money, our allegiances, and our all, to follow Him.

So many times God has been portrayed as a big Santa Claus, and all we have to do is confess and demand of Him new houses, cars, land and other material things, and we will automatically have them. We see people claiming houses, cars and other things, but very few claiming souls for God's kingdom.

True Wealth

The Bible speaks that we are to seek the true riches, not the riches of this world. His riches are things that money cannot buy. How can money deliver a wayward teenager from drugs and sin? How can money buy peace in our souls in the face of the fear all about us? How can money keep a marriage together? How can money bring healing to a dying person? How can money save a soul from hell? God's riches are available to do these things, but claiming the riches of the world will never accomplish them.

Certainly God does want to bless us with material things, but it will be Him that we are seeking when these things come, not the things. Many today are seeking God for what He can do for them, instead of seeking God asking what they can do for Him. **Matthew 6:31-33** tells us, **Therefore take no thought, saying, What shall we eat? or, What shall we drink? or, Wherewithal shall we be clothed? (For after all these things do the Gentiles seek:) for your heavenly Father knoweth that ye hath need of all these things. But seek ye first the kingdom of God, and his righteousness; and all these things shall be added unto you.**

The Lord tells us here to take no thought as to what we shall eat, drink, or wear. If we are to take no thought about these things, then should we go around claiming them? Certainly it is all right to ask God for our daily needs as our Lord prayed in the model prayer in **Matthew 6:11, Give us this day our daily bread.** However, our main emphasis should be upon seeking God's kingdom and praying for material things needed that would advance that kingdom.

Jesus said if we seek Him and His kingdom first, and His righteousness, then we will suffer no lack. We are told to be more concerned about having God's righteousness in us than about material things. If we want to claim something in our prayers, we need to claim His cleansing in our hearts, deliverance from all that offends Him, forgiveness for those that hurt us and that His nature be formed in us. If we are doing these things, He will supply materially for us in a beautiful way. He knows we have need of the things of the world because we live in this world. He wants to bless us with these things, even as we like to give our children gifts and take care of them.

Satan usually has people go from one extreme to another. Some he has claiming money, houses, cars, etc. (of course, always in the name of Jesus and for His kingdom, or else he could not convince people that it was right). Others he robs by telling them they do not deserve anything nice and that it is sinful to want nice things. Both extremes are not of our Lord.

Jesus says in the preceding verses that God clothes the grass of the field and the lilies, and that even Solomon and all his splendor was not arrayed as one of the lilies, so how much more shall he clothe us. He not only gives us physical clothing, but also he clothes us spiritually, so that others can see the joy of the Lord on our faces and His glow about us.

Our emphasis should always be on Jesus and what He wants for us; never should it be on the things we want from God. The most important thing in the sight of the Lord is our relationship with Him. We should seek Him about every problem and ask what His will is regarding each situation by giving up our way, and asking God for His way in the matter.

Our prayer should be, "Father, here I am; I give myself to You, my body, my family, my home, my ambitions, my social standing, my material possessions, my business, my dreams, and my plans. I withhold nothing from You. I am willing to part with anything that You say must go. I am willing to go any place You would send me; I am willing to stay any place You want me to stay. If You want me to give money to anyone of Your choosing, I am available. If You want me to leave my home and preach the gospel, I am willing. Should You desire me to stay right here in this unpleasant situation the rest of my days, I am willing. Father, whatever You request of me I will do, even though my flesh is not willing. Father, You know that I cannot do any of these things without Your grace and Your strength, so I depend on You for the power to do the things You ask of me, and to overcome the weakness of my flesh. Yes, Father, if You want me to take a particular job, I'm willing even though my flesh does not want to do so. I am presenting myself as a living sacrifice to You. Everything is up to You, Father. If this is the right person for me to marry, then I will. However, if they are not the right one, then no matter how much emotion I have for them, I ask You to remove it and take this person out of my life. Lord, I accept Your decisions in all matters, as You have perfect judgment and a perfect plan for my life. I trust You always to help me make the right decisions."

Commitment to God

In every situation that you and I face, we need to be willing to do whatever the Lord thinks best for us. This is what it means to be totally committed to His will. He sees the future and He knows better than we what is the best for us.

We are tempted to hold on to our "things," thinking they provide security for us at that moment. However, "things" change, and many times the very things we hold on to by refusing to give them to the Lord are lost anyway. Satan, the robber and thief, gains access to them because they do not belong to God. The only safe place for the things we love is in the hands of the Lord. If they belong to Him, then the devil has no right to them. If they do not, then Satan can ravage them.

If the Lord asks us to let go of anything, it is because it would be harmful for us, not just because He wants to deny us something. He wants to give us something better. His riches are beyond the things of this world.

John 12:24-26 states,

Verily, verily, I say unto you, Except a corn of wheat fall into the ground and die, it abideth alone: but if it die, it bringeth forth much fruit. He that loveth his life shall lose it; and he that hateth his life in this world shall keep it unto life eternal. If any man serve me, let him follow me; and where I

am, there shall also my servant be: if any man serve me, him will my Father honor.

It is always hard to die to our way of living and surrender to His; yet that is what is required of us if we are to truly live.

Most of us commit our lives by degree; we give God certain things, but others we hold back. This is not full committal and will never produce much fruit. It may produce thirtyfold, or even sixtyfold fruit, but never hundredfold fruit. Many people do make a commitment to God and He blesses them abundantly. However, they are unwilling to give up what the Lord has blessed them with, not realizing that their commitment to God is not a one-time experience. It is a daily commitment and dying to self.

God sometimes blesses with beautiful ministries, but often people make them their own, refusing to give them back to the Lord, saying that God gave it to them. The only reason God wants it back is to refine it, add something more to it, and then give it back in an even more beautiful way. So many hold on to the things that God gives them, refusing to give them back and so eventually end up losing them. In the kingdom of God the way to receive is to give. We must give Him our lives if we want to live.

The Author's Testimony

The two most difficult things for me to surrender have been in the areas where I have been blessed the most. I did not want to live alone nor be a missionary. My hesitance to give these to the Lord stemmed from a warped image of God. I was afraid He would ask me to do something that I did not want to do and that I would end up being miserable serving Him. Fear keeps many of us from receiving the blessings of God.

I felt a call on my life to serve God in a full-time ministry. I belonged to a church that allowed women to preach or teach only on foreign mission fields. I was afraid that God would ask me to go to a desolate foreign field and sit in a mud hut amid filth and poverty and preach His word to the natives. The other fear I had was that perhaps He would require me to be a female "Paul" and never marry. (I was single at the time and I did not want to live alone for the rest of my life.)

The Holy Spirit dealt with me so lovingly and patiently and brought me to the place where I could finally say, "All right, Lord, if you want me to be a missionary, I am willing; and if you want me to live alone for the rest of my days I will do that also. But, Lord, you know that I cannot do it without you; if you will give me the grace and strength to do it, I will." When I finally made this commitment, the Lord baptized me in the Holy Spirit.

I felt myself being filled with love, joy and peace that I had not known in my previous Christian walk. I felt a welling up in my Spirit, and out of my mouth came words in an unknown tongue. I found myself speaking in the spirit and it was one of the most wonderful experiences I had ever had. This experience was the one spoken about by Jesus in **John 7:37-39**:

In the last day, that great day of the feast, Jesus stood and cried, saying, If any man thirst, let him come unto me and drink. He that believeth on me, as the scripture hath said, out of his belly shall flow rivers of living water. (But this spake he of the Spirit, which they that believe on him should receive: for the Holy Ghost was not yet given; because that Jesus was not yet glorified.)

It is also spoken of in **Acts 1:4-8**:

And, being assembled together with them, commanded them that they should not depart from Jerusalem, but wait for the promise of the Father, which, saith he, ye have heard of me. For John truly baptized with water; but ye shall be baptized with the Holy Ghost not many days hence...But ye shall receive power, after that the Holy Ghost is come upon you: and ye shall be witnesses unto me both in Jerusalem, and in all Judea, and in Samaria, and unto the uttermost part of the earth.

Acts 2:4, And they were all filled with the Holy Ghost, and began to speak with other tongues, as the Spirit gave

them utterance. As I experienced this wonderful feeling of power, I grasped for the first time in my life a tremendous truth.

I knew in that moment that it did not matter if I lived in a mud hut or a mansion; it did not matter if I lived alone or was married. The only thing that really mattered was that His Spirit was in me. I knew in that moment that as long as He was with me in the mud hut I would be happy, and that if I were in a mansion without Him I would be miserable. I knew that I could live alone if I had Him. I also knew even a marriage would not work without Him. I understood that it was not my circumstances that created this joy I was feeling, but that it was solely the presence of the Holy Spirit. The only thing that mattered to me in that moment was Him. Since that day He has been my all-consuming love and life. I would choose no other path than the one that I have walked with Him. I found that the will of God was not being in a specific place at a specific time, but rather was having my heart set on doing His will. By following Him, I then would be where He wanted me, when He wanted me there.

I have since gone on missionary journeys and have been blessed beyond words. I lived without a mate for eight years before the Lord sent Bud into my life, and those years were as blessed as the years we have had together. The real blessing is having the Lord, not whom I am with, nor where I am. God did not lead me to remain permanently on a foreign field. However, I would be happy to serve Him there if He called.

I did not know God would use women in His work to preach and prophesy, but he confirmed this to me in **Acts 2:17-18**:

And it shall come to pass in the last days, saith God, I will pour out of my Spirit upon all flesh: and your sons and your daughters shall prophesy, and your young men shall see visions, and your old men shall dream dreams: And on my servants and on my handmaidens I will pour out in those days of my Spirit; and they shall prophesy. I am grateful and humbled to be called of God. I can truly say with the Psalmist David, **I delight to do thy will, O my God (Psalm 40:8)**. I did not delight in His will until He did an extensive work within me and renewed my carnal mind and worldly ways.

The Renewed Mind

After we have fully committed our lives to the Lord, we are told in **Romans 12** not to be conformed to this world, but to be transformed by the renewing of our minds. Only then can we prove what the good, acceptable, and perfect will of God is. Our carnal minds have been filled with the ways of the world for years before we came to the Lord, so it takes awhile to renew them to know the will of God. Plus, we were born carnal.

In **Romans 12**, He is saying that we are not to be governed by our ideas about any given situation, but we are to seek the Lord as to how He wants us to handle it. When we are seeking God's will, we should not ask the Lord to bless our plans, but rather ask to have the mind of Christ on the matter. If we are not walking in the spirit and do not know enough of the Word of God, we will automatically be ruled by the old carnal mind. Since our natural mind is filled with past ideas and is preprogrammed to think the way the world thinks, it can receive the wrong answer unless it is brought into submission to the Holy Spirit.

When confronted with a problem our prayer should be, "Father, I do not want my carnal mind to interfere with this decision; I want the mind of Christ to guide and direct me. Father, if you will reveal your will to me, I will obey you, even if it is not what I desire to do as I trust your guidance."

The reason we make so many wrong decisions is that we do not know the mind of the Lord and what the Word of God says about each situation. For example, if a doctor says that we have a fatal disease and we do not know that the Word of God says, "By His stripes we are healed," we will believe the doctor's diagnosis and die. We receive the things we believe. I am not coming specifically against medical knowledge here, as doctors view things from their perspective and teaching and from what they perceive to be facts. However, there is a higher knowledge and a Greater Physician who can heal all diseases, and if we go to Him we can be healed.

Coming from a medical background myself, I have had a real struggle to cast down the carnal mind and put on the mind of Christ in situations where I knew, medically speaking, that it was impossible for someone to be healed. However, I knew that in God nothing is impossible. The "spirit man" in me believed this stronger than my carnal mind doubted; therefore I could pray with confidence for healing and see the Lord perform miracles. Some of us, in time, may be faced with the choice of believing what the doctors tell us or what the Spirit of God tells us in His Word. We must trust God and not our minds.

But the natural man receiveth not the things of the Spirit of God: for they are foolishness unto him: neither can he know them, because they are spiritually discerned. But he that is spiritual judgeth all things, yet he himself is judged of no man. For who hath known the mind of the Lord, that he may instruct him? But we have the mind of Christ (1 Corinthians 2:14-16).

This does not mean we are not to go to doctors, but rather keep our trust in God and not in them, as they have limited knowledge. At this writing, I have personally not had to go to a medical doctor for treatment for the past twenty years. I testify to this with gratefulness and humility. I am not exalting myself but rather my great God who made this testimony possible. I have had several attacks of sickness and infirmities over the years; however, through standing on my covenant promises and by prayer I was healed each time. Doctors are limited, God is unlimited!

In ten years of weekly church services (with meetings two and three times weekly) plus ten years of evangelistic services I have never missed a service due to illness save one service in the very beginning of the ministry. I was just then learning how to believe God for healing. The Lord God is faithful to His Word and He gets the credit for this testimony!

The original publishing of this book did not contain this testimony as I wanted to be sure this was shared for God's glory and not in a prideful manner. **Psalms 105:1, I give thanks unto the Lord; call upon his name: make known his deeds among the people. Psalm 75:1, Unto thee, O god, do we give thanks, unto thee do we give thanks: for that thy name is near thy wondrous works declare.**

We renew our minds by reading and meditating on the Word of God and by fellowshipping with the Father. Then, if a crisis comes we can be victorious, for we will have the mind of the Lord. We must consistently put the Word of God in our minds and ask God to cleanse us from all things that are not of Him.

In times past, we have filled our minds with television, secular magazines, newspaper articles and the local gossip. All of these things produce death and we cannot expect to know the will of God when these are the seeds we are sowing in our minds. Our TV screens are filled with violence, sin and "trash;" our newspapers foster fear and depression; our magazines create lustful desires for the things of this world, and our conversations can be negative and destructive. Is it any wonder that we have no spiritual strength or godly wisdom and guidance when this is what we have been putting into our minds? If we spent the same time with the Lord and His Word we would soon not only be able to discern His will, but also be able to walk therein.

Walking in His Will

We are told in **Romans 12:2** to prove what God's will is. How do we prove whether something is His will or not? We check it out with the Word of God. If it does not agree with His word, it is not His will. We are told to prove what is that good and acceptable and perfect will of God. In looking at this verse we need to notice that this is not speaking of three separate pathways of God's will, but is speaking of one will of God that is good, acceptable and perfect.

31

At one time, I thought this was referring to three different paths. I was concerned that perhaps I was only in His acceptable will. I wanted to be in His perfect will. Maybe it meant that if I got out of one path, I would end up on a lower one. Or perhaps I had missed God and would forever remain on the acceptable path, and it could not be corrected because of some decision made years ago in my life.

Some people are deceived into believing that the mate they were married to before they were saved is only in the acceptable will of God for them as the marriage took place before they knew the Lord. This is a terrible lie of the devil. God desires to take that mate and make him perfect, not to do away with him. They are not meant to swap mates for a Christian one, or swap situations just to have relief for themselves. God wants them to believe for their mates, not cast them away.

The will of God is one path, not three. The Lord revealed this to me in a vision as I was contemplating this Scripture. He showed me a vision of a pathway stretching out in front of me. As I approached the path I noticed that it was very broad at its beginning, gradually narrowing until finally at the end it became very narrow. The Lord then explained this pathway.

He said, "When you are 'born again' you step into My will and enter into a very broad place. At the beginning of My will the boundaries are very broad and liberal. You can wander from one side of the path to the other, which is a considerable distance, and still not be out of My will. You have entered into My acceptable will. I accept you just as you are. You may have many faults and sins when you come to Me, but I receive you and accept you. It is not your place to struggle with your sins, but it is My place to remove those sins as you give them to me. As we walk together down the pathway of My will, I will cleanse you from those sins and make the changes within that you desire."

He then showed me as we continued that the path began to narrow. Consequently, there was not as much room to wander as at the beginning. I then knew that as He began to do a good work in me, I was then more restricted in the things that I could and could not do. He now did not allow many things that I used to do, as He was leading me more into Himself.

Being confident of this very thing, that he which hath begun a good work in you will perform it until the day of Jesus Christ (Philippians 1:6).

As I continued down the path it became very narrow, so that if I took one step in either direction, I would be off the path. I realized then I had entered into His perfect will, not that I was perfect, but that He was leading me in a perfect way so that I could become perfect. I realized this was the place that the Scripture referred to in **Matthew 7:13-14, Enter ye in at the strait gate: for wide is the gate, and broad is the way, that leadeth to destruction, and many there be which go in thereat: Because strait is the gate, and narrow is the way, which leadeth unto life, and few there be that find it**.

In this walk we can see the thirtyfold Christians who stay at the broad place; others we find who will walk farther with the Lord and produce sixtyfold fruit, but so few who will enter the strait and narrow and produce fruit a hundredfold, with the results of perfection being manifested in their lives.

As I approached the end of this path, we came to a very narrow gate. When it was opened, I was surprised to see a beautiful field in front of me with rolling hills and brooks, a very wide open space. Here was the reward for the sons of God, a place of freedom, not restriction.

Once we have been trained and cleansed, the Lord then bestows much freedom upon us. We can choose the things we would do and receive the things we desire. Our choices at this point will not hurt others for we will be as Paul, who said in **1 Corinthians 6:12, All things are lawful unto me, but all things are not expedient: all things are lawful for me, but I will not be brought under the power of any**. With God we will walk through the acceptable, the good, and the perfect, planting seeds and bearing fruit, until we come into that hundredfold production where the life of Christ continually flows through us. Not only will we know His will, but we will be His will because we will have been transformed into His image. **...that ye may stand perfect and complete in all the will of God (Colossians 4:12). We know that whosoever is born of God sinneth not; but he that is begotten of God keepeth himself, and that wicked one toucheth him not. (1 John 5:18).**

To know God's will we must not only be committed to God and transformed by His power, but also something else is required. **Verse 3 of Romans 12** says, **For I say, through the grace given unto me, to every man that is among you, not to think of himself more highly than he ought to think; but to think soberly, according as God hath dealt to every man the measure of faith.**

When we approach God seeking His will, we must remain humble before him and not think of ourselves more highly than we ought. We come before Him as a little child with a meek spirit seeking Him for our answers, knowing we have no answers outside of Him. If we come as a little child (childlike, not childish), the Lord will show us what to do. Little children look to their parents with a trusting heart for their answers, and we should come to the Father with the same attitude.

Spiritual Pride

Many people have fallen because of spiritual pride. What is spiritual pride? It is pride and trust in one's own knowledge of God's Word, instead of childlike trust in God. The focal point has shifted from God to the things of God. Some people think they have all the answers and that they have come so far that it is now impossible to be wrong. They tend to base everything on past victories in the Lord. Paul warned against this in 1 **Corinthians 9:27, But I keep under my body, and bring it into subjection: lest that by any means, when I have preached to others, I myself should be a castaway.**

We can become prideful (boastful) in our faith or in our answers to prayers. This sin of spiritual pride is so deadly because it is not as evident as the pride and egotism of the world. It produces faith in our faith instead of faith in God. We need to remember it is the object of our faith that produces results, not our amount of faith. Faith can produce answers, but without love it profits nothing. **1 Corinthians 13:2 says: And though I have the gift of prophecy, and understand all mysteries, and all knowledge; and though I have all faith, so that I could remove mountains, and have not charity, I am nothing**.

We must humbly and respectfully seek the Lord for His answers, and not trust in our own. If we really want to know God's will, we must approach Him with a spirit of humility. The greatest danger in gaining knowledge is that **...Knowledge puffeth up, but charity edifieth. And if any man think that he knoweth anything, he knoweth nothing yet as he ought to know (1 Corinthians 8:1-2)**.

We sometimes seek God for an answer so that we can boast to others that we have heard from God. We must continually be diligent to resist the spirit of pride and boastfulness. This spirit can come against us whether we are just a baby in the Lord or an older saint. When we receive truths that others have not yet received, we should be most loving in presenting them, or we can become a proud spiritual peacock.

Perhaps we have received the truths of the baptism in the Holy Spirit, speaking in tongues and healing; yet if we look down on those that have not received these spiritual truths, we offend them and keep them from coming into this knowledge. We should remember that we did not always have this light ourselves. The Lord loves us all, no matter where we are in Him.

Love is always the door through which others will walk into these truths. We must remember this as we share our knowledge. We must not only approach the Lord with a humble spirit, but also must present His truths to others with that same spirit of meekness.

Paul says in **Romans 12:3** that we are not only to be humble, but also that we are to think soberly, according as God has dealt to every man the measure of faith. When we are asking God for a direction, or seeking His wisdom and His will, we are also to deal with the problem through sober thinking. Faith is not opposed to our minds.

God gave us a mind, and through it comes our knowledge of Him. It is only the carnal mind that is enmity against God. That is the mind of this world. God wants us to have a new mind in Him that is free from Satan's influence. When we receive God's will on any given subject, if we have truly committed it to the Lord and are willing to obey Him, we will find our mind in agreement with God's direction. It will seem reasonable to us.

God is a logical God, and He will not ask of us illogical things. He may sometimes request something that we may not fully understand, but we will have a peace in our heart about it, and our mind will agree to it. Some people have been deceived in this area when they thought God was speaking something unreasonable to them. They later admitted they knew it was illogical, but at the time felt God was testing their faith. God does not require things of us that our faith cannot handle. He said to be sober-minded according to our faith. If you don't have faith for walking on water, don't walk on it just because Peter did. Jesus spoke to Peter and said, "Come." If it is not the Lord speaking the command for us to come, then we will drown.

Many people do illogical things in the name of the Lord, when He is not calling or leading them at all. For instance, God would not call a mother of ten children to leave them and go to the mission field. She has a mission field at home. Our God is a logical God.

If He does call you to do something that sounds impossible, He will equip you and give you the faith and peace to do it. He makes provision for all He asks of us. If we have thought a certain direction to be of God, but, after obeying we see no provision being made, it would be well for us to look closely to see if it is really the Lord who is leading. We are to approach things not only from the faith viewpoint, but also from a logical, sober-minded viewpoint as well. God will not call us to one thing while we are neglecting others. He will not call us to abandon our families and leave them without care, but rather will expand our capabilities not only to care for them, but also to do His work. He will send people to help us as our work load grows for Him.

If we approach God for an answer as to His will, we certainly must not leave out the ingredient of coming by faith. We must believe that He is going to give us an answer when we ask Him for one. It is futile to ask and then think that He will not answer. We must believe by faith that we are going to receive.

Our answers can come in many forms. He can speak audibly; however, this is admittedly an exceptional manner. Or, as He generally does, He can speak to us through His Spirit within us. It will be a "knowing," with a peace about the situation. He also speaks to us through His Word. As we meditate on His Word, He can "quicken" (cause to come alive) a certain verse that will be our answer. Many times He will bring a Scripture to our minds that will direct us. Sometimes we can receive our answers from a book, or we might hear a teaching or sermon that contains what we need to hear. The Lord can even have someone speak the answer to us. The Lord has many ways of sending an answer if we are sincerely looking for it to come and are believing by faith that we will receive it.

Praise God that He is alive and on His throne and that He does hear and answer our prayers! We do not have to go down the wrong roads and learn the hard way. We can diligently seek God and He will answer us, and thus save us from many pitfalls. Many trials and tribulations could be avoided if we diligently sought the Lord before we started out in what we believed to be the right way. The Lord never demands that we make quick decisions involving major changes in our lives. We need to seek Him carefully before we "launch out."

Knowing God's will is not an automatic thing. It takes trust, obedience, study, prayer, seeking and a total commitment to God. There are no easy "Seven Steps to Victory." Only a daily walk with God, fellowshipping with Him, will bring that victory. There are no pat answers, and no book that will bring us those answers (outside of the Bible). This book is no exception. It is designed to give you the tools so that you may find the answers for yourself. In the final analysis, Jesus is the only answer for each of us. As we get to know Him better and learn to follow in His steps, we will ultimately walk into our answer.

A number of years ago, the Lord awakened me in the night and spoke to me to write down the following words. I share this prophetic poem with you in love. As you read it may the Holy Spirit minister to your heart as He did mine:

The Steps of My Son
(as inspired by the Holy Spirit)

Accept My leading in all you do.
Listen for My guidance as I call you.
There are times you will not know where to turn
But as you look to Me, My voice you will learn.
I am ever present, now and through eternity.
The efforts you make will be blessed by Me.
Wait now, hearken to My word,
I will tell you things you have not heard.
For there are secrets revealed by Me,
But they are only seen and discerned spiritually.
Obey My Spirit as gently I speak
It comes not to the wise, but to the meek.
All true wisdom comes through Me.
Search and you will find if you discard vanity,
For My power and wisdom come only as you die,
The same way My Son received, that's to crucify.
Unto subjection the flesh must be brought
Dying to self, that's what Jesus taught.

But, oh, so few find this way because they seek
Honor and glory, but refuse the way of the meek.
All that I give comes by death,
For then it is reborn, given life and breath.
Yes, born of My Spirit, it is made anew
Your life a sacrifice, tried and true.
You must be buried, as a grain of corn
To see the fruit of My Spirit born.
Absolute surrender is what I require
Then, you may have the things you desire.
The first time you come to the cross, I give to you
Birth of your spirit and life, brand new.
But the second time, it is your turn to give
You must give Me your life, if you want to live.
A surrendered vessel, I work through
Yes, My chosen ones, I want all of you.
As you yield, old things will pass away and you will find
I will create within you a new heart and mind.
You will look back then and wonder why
You waited so long to finally die.
Yes, death to your way and surrender to Me
Fulfillment and happiness, they are yours, you see.
The way to declare the victory won--
Comes, only as you follow the steps of My Son.

1 Peter 2:21: For even hereunto were ye called: because Christ also suffered for us, leaving us an example, that ye should follow his steps.

Index

L

Learning by hearing and obeying 15
Learning by trial and error 15, 16, 37

M

Meekness 35

N

New Birth 4

O

Overcoming 5, 9, 10, 11, 17, 18, 19, 21, 24

P

Paul's thorn in the flesh 12, 16, 17, 18
Poverty and the Christian 8, 19
Prayer 3, 5, 6, 7, 9, 22, 23, 24, 29, 30, 35, 37, 38
Prayers, answered 4, 5, 20, 30
Prophecies, proving 2

R

Resist the devil 8, 9, 14, 35
Righteousness, God's in the Christian 15, 23
Ruling and reigning with Christ 10

S

Salvation is God's will 6, 9
Self-will, dying to 21

Postnote

The Millers are very glad to receive mail from their readers; however, they are unable to answer the letters personally due the volume of mail that they receive. They will be happy to pray along with their intercessors for all who write with a prayer request; although they do no outside counseling as they believe this should be directed to local pastors as outlined in Scripture.

Christ Unlimited Ministries, Inc. is a non-profit church 501(c) (3) corporation. All contributions are tax deductible. We appreciate your prayers, encouragement and support. Your purchase of this book makes it possible for us to share free copies of Bibles, teaching literature, tracts and downloadable audio/video materials with ministers in third world countries who would otherwise not be able to purchase them.

The Lord gave the word: great was the company of those that published it (Psalm 68:11).

For Additional Study

This book is taken from a course of Bible studies called the Overcoming Life Series. The entire series is a virtual "spiritual tool chest," as it covers a multitude of subjects every Christian faces in his walk with God. It also answers questions that many believers have concerning the current move of God. These are dealt with in a balanced approach and in the light of the Scripture. God's people are not to live frustrated, defeated lives, but rather they are to be victorious overcomers! Other books available with their companion workbooks are:

PROVE ALL THINGS - Christ warned that great deception would be one of the signs of the end times. In this book, instruction is given on how to recognize false prophets and teachings. Clear Scriptural guidelines are given on discerning the Spirit of truth versus the spirit of error. The book deals with how to judge without being judgmental.

THE TRUE GOD - This is a teaching on the character of God, explaining why God does certain things, and why it is against His nature to do other things. It differentiates between the things for which God is responsible and the things for which the devil is responsible. Our responsibility as Christians destined to overcome is made clear so that we can live victorious lives.

THE WILL OF GOD - This lesson teaches us not only how to know the will of God in our personal lives, family, ministry and finances, but also brings understanding as to why God allows sin, sickness and suffering in the world. As overcomers, Christians are not to suffer under many of the things we have accepted as normal.

KEYS TO THE KINGDOM - Instruction on how to gain authority in God's Kingdom through prayer is the topic of this book. Many principles and methods of prayer are covered, such as praying in the Spirit, fasting and prayer, travailing prayer, praise, intercession and spiritual warfare.

EXPOSING SATAN'S DEVICES - This book is a powerful expose' of Satan's tricks, tactics and lies. Cult and Occultic methods and groups are listed so Christians can detect their activity. Demon activity is discussed and deliverance and casting out demons is dealt with in detail. Satan's kingdom is uncovered and the Christian is taught to overcome through spiritual discernment and warfare.

HEALING OF THE SPIRIT, SOUL AND BODY - This book teaches how to overcome emotional problems, as well as physical ones, and how to receive divine healing. It also teaches how to renew the carnal mind and walk in the spirit of life, thereby overcoming depression, loneliness and fear.

NEITHER MALE NOR FEMALE - What is the woman's role in the church and home? Who is a woman's spiritual head and covering? Does God call women to the five-fold ministry? What does God's Word say about divorce, celibacy and choosing a marriage partner? These and other woman related topics are Scripturally examined.

EXTREMES OR BALANCE? - Many Christians have hurt the cause of Christ through "out-of-balance" teachings and demonstrations. This book shows how to avoid those areas. It also deals wisely with the excesses and extremes in the body of Christ.

THE PATHWAY INTO THE OVERCOMER'S WALK - This book contains answers to the questions an overcomer faces as he presses toward the prize of the high calling in Christ Jesus. How can we be conformed to the image of Christ? How does the Holy Spirit work with the overcomers in the end times? What are the overcomer's rewards?

PERSONAL SPIRITUAL WARFARE - Explains the invisible world of spiritual forces that influence our lives and how good can prevail over the evil around us as we prepare for the new kingdom age that is coming. This book will help you overcome problems in your finances, marriage, the emotional pressures of fear, anger and hurt. Here are the keys to victory through spiritual warfare.

MARK OF GOD OR MARK OF THE BEAST - Much has been written and said about the mark of the beast, but little has been said about the mark of God. What does the 666 mean and what is this mysterious mark? How is it linked to the world of finance? Has this mark already begun? This book answers many questions about the mark of the beast and the mark of God, and how they affect Christians.

Please visit our web site for information on how to order the complete "Overcoming Life Bible Study." Our site is also an excellent source for additional books and Bible resources.

http://www.BibleResources.org

Purpose and Vision

Go ye therefore, and teach all nations, baptiz-
ing them in the name of the Father, and of the Son,
and of the Holy Ghost: Teaching them to observe
all things whatsoever I have commanded you: and,
lo, I am with you alway, even unto the end of the
world. Amen.

Matthew 28:19,20

Christ Unlimited is not "another denomination," sect, or just
a separate group. It is an arm of the Body of Christ — the Church
of Jesus Christ, which has been called to strengthen the Body at
large. We also believe we have been called to help establish the
Kingdom of God in the earth.

Christ Unlimited is involved with all Bible-believing Christians regardless of their church or denominational affiliations and
committed to helping wherever possible in evangelistic and teaching outreaches.

Christ Unlimited believes that time is running out and the
Gospel has not been preached to every creature. Many nations
have not heard the Gospel, and in many places, doors for evange-
lism are closing. We believe it is time all Christians cooperated
with the Lord in breaking down denominational walls for a united
front line against the kingdom of darkness and in setting up the
Kingdom of the Lord Jesus Christ by the power of the Holy Spirit.

Christ Unlimited provides such tools as to enable the saints
of God to establish the Kingdom of God in the earth. We encour-
age groups of prayer warriors who will pray, fast, and intercede
for the nations. This, we believe, is weapon number one. We teach
believers how to overcome through spiritual warfare and through

49

knowing how to use their authority in Christ Jesus through the Word and the power of the Holy Spirit.

Christians need to know how to bring down the forces of darkness in their own lives and in the lives of those to whom they minister. We provide such tools as Bibles, literature, Christ Unlimited books and an online prayer ministry. We publish the Gospel going out via any means of communication; including the internet, videos, as well as literature. We have teaching seminars, Bible schools, and correspondence courses, all aimed at winning souls to Christ and building the Body of Christ into maturity.

Bud and Betty Miller serve the Lord together as founders of the multi-visioned ministry outreach, Christ Unlimited. The outreaches of this ministry have stemmed from a tremendous desire to see the Word of God taught in its balanced entirety. The Millers are firm believers in prayer and, through prayer, have seen many released from the bondages of fear, failure, and defeat.

The outreaches of Christ Unlimited are in obedience to the words of our Lord in **Mark 16:15**: **Go ye into all the world and preach the gospel to every creature.** This mandate from the Lord presents a challenge to our generation as an estimated 25 percent of the world's population still have not heard the Good News of Jesus Christ.

Christ Unlimited Ministries also is dedicated to teaching God's Word. **Hosea 4:6** says: **My people are destroyed for lack of knowledge.** Many Christians are leading defeated lives simply because they do not know God's Word in its fullest.

Christ Unlimited Ministries has provided for those who desire to know God's Word in a greater way. The main thrust of the teaching and literature is directed at "How to be an overcomer." In the endtimes, we must be prepared to overcome the onslaughts of Satan. Many Christians are suffering needlessly, because they do not know how to overcome sickness, depression, divorce, fear, and financial failure. Christ Unlimited Ministries provides answers for troubled families as well as trains workers for service.